The Sound of Solace

An Anthology Curated by

Kavya Tandon

Inkfeathers Publishing
www.inkfeathers.com

The Sound of Solace
Edited & Compiled by Kavya Tandon
Print Edition

First Published in India in 2022
Inkfeathers Publishing
New Delhi 110095

Copyright © Inkfeathers Publishing, 2022

ISBN 9789390882144

www.inkfeathers.com

For you, Karbon;

you were and continue to be my solace.

Disclaimer

The anthology 'The Sound of Solace' is a collection of 46 poems and 2 short stories written by 35 authors who belong to different parts of the world.

Unless otherwise indicated, all the names, characters, objects, businesses, places, events, incidents- whether physical/non-physical, real/unreal, tangible/ intangible in whatsoever description used in this book are either the product of the author's imagination or used in a fictitious manner. Any resemblance to actual persons, objects, entities, living or dead, or actual events is purely coincidental.

The poems & stories published in this book are solely owned by their respective authors and are in no way intended to hurt anyone's religious, political, spiritual, brand, personal or fanatic beliefs and/or faith, whatsoever. In case, any sort of plagiarism is detected in the contents within this anthology or in case of any complaints, grievances, or objections, neither the anthology editor nor the publisher is to be held responsible.

Featuring the writings of

Deborah Mejía, Czarina Datiles, Pratishtha Jindal

Ramaponni P, Tanmay Agrawal, Sage, Anisha Jain

Mitali Kushwaha, Deepika Kumari, Rashi Sadhu

Vivek Chowthri, Hrishita Sood, Dr. Arun Kumar Shastri

Anju Kurien, Arshpreet Kaur, Md Adnan, Rohit Agrawal

Akanksha Badu, Sidharath Ghassi, Ishani Mitra

Zubaida Ifshan, Mahek Patel, Anindita Chatterjee

Riya Prasad, Ishita Rawat, Riya Om, Sharon Paul

Akhila James, Anagha Gopan O.G., Abhisha Gulati

Ammarah Safaa, Hiya Shah, Deepti Chauhan

Zahistha Begum, Anushka Jain

Contents

About the Editor

Kavya Tandon

Kavya Tandon is a twenty-year-old Economics student who is on a mission to ensure education for all. She firmly believes that when it comes to education, no one should be left behind, which led her to start her non-profit organisation, Project Adhyayan. In her free time, she can be found reading and writing poetry attacking the social evils prevalent in society.

Editor's Note

In recent years, all of us have faced increasing mental pressures and had to live through a deadly pandemic. We as a society have realised the importance of living life and not just surviving; we realised the importance of solitude, of solace. Comfort comes in all forms, giving us hope in our darkest days. 'The Sound of Solace' acts as a beacon of hope in times such. It helped me, the co-authors and by extension, I'm hoping, you to find our comfort places, places we look forward to. This book brought us together, bound us by this bond of acceptance and peace and we hope this bond engulfs you too, and helps you breathe a little easier, smile a little more.

So, dear reader, come be a part of this little comfort circle. Read our journeys—our ups and downs, our laughter, and sorrows—but most importantly, our hope.

With this, a little piece of my heart is forever yours. This book acted as my escape in my toughest hours, and this is what I'm sharing with you, hoping to cheer you up when you're low and share your laughter when you feel ecstatic.

Now and forever yours,
Kavya Tandon

Sing a song for me

Czarina Datiles

I know this is selfish of me to ask
But would you sing a song for me?
Tell the canary to hum a small tune
Tell the grass to orchestrate a melody
Tell the winds to serenade the lyrics
You wrote
Of sunshine, flowers, and summer bees.

You see,
It's too quiet in this vega
Between breath and death
Where the only chirps I hear
Are the crows of warning
And the only plants here
Are lilies of mourning.
Time passes slowly
In this world of opal and midnight blues
It's lonely to be living
When all who's with you
is simply you.

A life full of hustle and bustle
Sprinting and reaching
       Enduring and existing
       For once, I feel like living
       Breathing
       As the sound of your chords
Strums my heart alive.
Feeling and seeing
What life is all about.

All I ask, my darling son,
Is for you to sing me a siren's charm
And melt my frozen soul with your warmth
Prepare me for Heaven
Or whatever world awaits this life.
Put a smile to my blue lips,
Put daisies on my sealed eyes,
And sing me a song loud enough
To make this passing phantom cry.
A song so delicate
       Like a blossom
A voice so raw
       That it bleeds
Sing me a song, my darling child
       So that I may leave
       This world
       In solace
       And in peace.

Vega (Spanish) – A beautiful grassland

Driving with the Music On

Zahistha Begum

Feeling high on the breeze,
Along with the high note, bleach.
All my misery away,
To let it sink by the sea bay.

Speed gradually taking a leap,
As the singer drowns in his weep,
Heart burning and rumbling,
To the deep notes of the drumming.

Dark and gloomy is the sky,
Just like the music's cry,
Tears welling in my eyes,
As I am moving forward by.

And here comes the destination,
Wondering if life is all but imagination.
But there is no stop and I let out a loud horn,
Because am ready to embrace, driving with the music on.

Confession of Daughter to Her Mother

Riya Om

Maa,
Since childhood, you were in my mind,
But I never felt that way,
The way I am feeling now.
Losing you was just another memory for me,
But now I feel that loss.
I cannot see your picture,
Just because I cannot handle my emotions,
But you know I love you.
I don't know your dreams for me,
I even did not get a chance to know you well,
But Mom, after all, I am your part,
And I know I am making you proud.
I always tried to find you in other women,
But Mom it's not easy.
I do have a person who loves me like you,
But still, I miss you.
I never understood,
Why people say a mother is a mother,
But I think now I can understand.
I really wish I could be able to feel you,

I could have done something for you.
Maa, I don't know where you are,
But sometimes, I try to find you in the stars,
Although I don't in this theory,
But you know sometimes I want to,
Sometimes I feel like you will come,
Like in TV shows, parents give surprises to their kids,
You also will,
I wish this could happen.

On a Drive

Pratishtha Jindal

When the water embraces
And creates a place—
Just for you,
And in that space
You build a world
Of your own,
Weightless, you float.
And the world
Simply breathes,
And exists.

I feel that calm
While driving through
This celestial road.
Watching the trees
And the sun
Dancing.
Our music,
Intertwined—
Our music,
Like remedy,

Creates a cured reality
That I have only
Dreamt.

Imagine,
You are here with me—
Hearing the wind
As it moves through
The open windows,
And gently sings.

The warmth in my chest
As I travel through
This dream
Is ethereal
And healing.
In every passing breath,
The world
Reminds me,
I'm real,
As real as this dream

Found

Pratishtha Jindal

When the world felt
Too cold
And my thoughts
Armed with
Carnivorous teeth,
I devised a retreat.
Without any sight
My hands traced the rough walls
And discovered a door
In my heart,
And to it, I reached out,
And there, I found you.
You—
Who inspires me to live,
You—
Who sings to me,
And fills the void of
A world—
That is either too quiet
Or too loud.

Entering this place
I allow myself to feel safe,
And the numbness
Of being lost
Dissipates.
See me?
If you close your eyes,
You will feel me.
I am the sunshine running
Wildly through the ripples
Of this quaint river,
Giggling like an untamed child.
This place,
I realised—
Exists eternally.
Unbound by the tangible reality.
It is sacred ground.
Here, I freely wear my skin
And my real face.
Navigating through the
Map of words you gave me,
I find myself again
Or rather, unhide and unveil.
Now, staring at me
Are all the known

And unknown
And indiscernible
Pieces of me.
In the galaxy of me,
I look at us,
Shining.
Me—
A star,
That felt insignificant
In the vast fabric of the night sky.
Recalls,
Seeing through
The melody of your eyes
The meaning of a star's light
The meaning
And preciousness
Of existing.

In a cold world,
In the rhythm of my heart
I found your silhouette
And you gave me faith,
That I will give myself
The best of me.
I found the answer
That was
Right in front of me.

Awake at Dawn

Pratishtha Jindal

Ashore at dawn,
I hear the nameless bird
Cry out its call.
Behind my eyes
I try to paint her wings
Soaring in the wind.
The sky—
Bidding to her call—
Slowly changes
From
The inky blues
To lighter hues.
I see—
Mesmerised,
As the colours of the day
Bloom.

I find myself marking a path
To greet the waves,
I find myself
Wishing to acquaint.
Reluctant to break the ethereal stillness,
We whisper quietly—
Talking about our travels,
Sharing our love for the moon and stars,
Recognising our reverence for the sun.

Then, as they get ready to depart
I ask them—
How could there be such beauty?
And they answer—
Because you are here to see,
Awake at dawn
Suddenly overcome with peace
Warmth settles and
Radiates from my chest.
I revere in the soft touch
Of the sand
Beneath my feet—
As I see the waves recede,
I see them be free.

Carving My Space

Pratishtha Jindal

The quiet night
Caresses the tiredness
Singing in my bones.

Laying out on my porch,
I see galaxies,
I am searching for fables
In the soft touch of grass
Beneath my skin.

I try to find the gaze
Of eyes I adore
In the startling light
Of stars
Shinning above my home.

My mind
Bruised with thoughts
I failed to escape.

I play music
And pray
For it to be
A remedy,

The melodies
And lyrics—
My medic.

The cold wind
Embraces the numbness
I once felt
And the hurt I still do,
It all becomes a part of me.

What was I even running from?
It's just me.

With a cup of tea warming my hands
I converse with flowers
And trees.
In their infinite wisdom,
They tell me
Secrets of existing.

On a serene sight—
I find myself,
Breathing.

Just Because I'm a girl

Rashi Sadhu

When I was in my mother's womb
I felt safe like a bloom.

As I stepped out into this world
Opened my eyes, I was so thrilled.

Finding myself wrapped in my mother's arms
Seeing my father brought within me a calm.

Being a girl, I was so glad
Yet some were happy, some were sad.

As I moved ahead of my life
The facade of this world made me horrified.

Deep inside I feel like a stereotype
In this complex world that makes everything hype.

I was devastated and my heart filled with pain.
My soul felt like it'll go insane.

This world is full of morons
Where I feel myself completely forlorn.

I have been taunted that I don't deserve.
They don't want me but just my curves.

Teardrops were running down, falling off my nose,
Crying in the dark corner, where nobody goes.

My eyes are telling story of my anger and pain
You think that I'm happy, just look again.

Painted with faux smile I'm a master of disguise
You can see it all just look into my eyes.

God has created me for purpose
Don't treat me like an object that is worthless.

Don't forget that you too have to end up there
Where you'll find nothing but hell everywhere.

I have boundless potential as great as light
All tucked in a body that itself creates life.

Girl has always been a real treasure
Whose true worth no one can ever measure.

Butterflies

Mahek Patel

Was stopped in my track,
By a scene so stunning,
A plethora of flowers with a butterfly dancing,
It felt as if nature was beckoning.

Had a blend of different shades,
With the dominance of white,
As colourful as a rainbow,
It was an absolute delight.

Soon came its companion,
Started circling around,
It was yet another beautiful creation,
Having an impact profound.

They lit up the place,
With their grace floating in the breeze,
Even better with the perfect lighting,
The fascination made me freeze.

Realisation dawned upon me,
Made me grab my bike,
It was time for us to go home,
Me and them alike.

Every time I feel lonely,
Or try to find solace,
The butterflies flutter before my eyes,
The sight becomes my happy place.

The Ocean

Hrishita Sood

Sitting by the side of an ocean
I wonder what life is
Then my gaze falls at the setting sun
Which reminds me how time flies
And it's just those little moments that are priceless

Life is about the ones who enter our lives
The same way how ships sail in the ocean
They are here until their purpose is fulfilled
And then they leave.

Life can also be about the choices we make
Some choices add meaning to our lives
And some are just about regrets.

It can even be about the thoughts
Which are more like the waves in the ocean
They hit the shore and go back
Same way as thoughts strikes the mind and then disappear.

Life is not just about ups and downs
But how we respond to them
The way how sandcastles on the beach
Respond to the waves.

Life is all about being happy
It's about finding your little corner
Amidst the chaos of this world
Which gives you solace!

My Canvas

Arshpreet Kaur

My canvas has different shades,
Some are faded and some are great.
It's my mezzanine which has an east face,
Having ample rays.

The yellow ball on the azure sky with a furrow of clouds,
In which birds are ready to dive.
The smoky road, has a jam, but a green patch
fills that black with flamboyant red.

The breezy wind, crossing hills, singing songs
And flocks of birds dancing with that.
Surprisingly, my canvas has sound effects.

Some little ones are sitting in their nest,
Watching and waiting for their turn.
Their chirping noise creates poise all around
As my canvas has an aural effect.

Look! Painter is trying to make something haze,
The colour pervades like a maze,
It seems clouds are on graze
and they cover the blaze.

Tiny drops at their edge, falling on the leaves,
Mingling with a gleam,
Shining like an abundance of gems.

Someone is peeping out of the curtains of mist,
It has a twist, like an arc
and having seven colourful marks.

Gradually, curtains are going to close
And dark colours are ready to blow.
I think Painter Has an ulterior motive here,
As it's dark but lots of twinkling dots are there,
Looking like someone is lighting millions of lamps.

One white, big, glowy sphere is also there,
Someone is playing and it has escaped from there.
This dimness has sturdiness, it is showing mightiness.

I am thinking about the painter,
Who has given beautiful strokes to that,
but someone is here,
Who is trying to spoil those shades?

My painter has painted completely,
Now it's on us, how we keep it safely.

A Green Corner

Arshpreet Kaur

There is a green corner in my den.
A green, lovely, charming corner escorted by roses red and
white along with pink hibiscus.
It always allures me, come, and sit with a cup of tea and have a
bliss with me.

Though we have a voiceless relation but never feel solitude
while we are together.
I can splurge my hours without saying something to you,
as I can babble without unzip my lips with you.

I think I am in deep love with you as I am an ardent lover of
you.
My love as deep as an ocean.
It is as pristine as a morning dew.

I can feel psithurism of you and that petrichor aroma makes me
wonderful aesthete of you.
Your every movement, teaches something to me, whether it's
sapling seeds, rustling of leaves,
infancy of buds, blooming of flowers or even those yellow leaves
which are ready to leave.

At times, I am in torpid state.
That time, I clung on you and love to see sapling seeds,
sprouting of leaves
and believe me it gives me zest and this moment is best, can't
express because words are less.

Infancy of buds shows emblem of a new beginning of life.
It shows nothing in the universe can stop me from letting go
and starting over a new life.

Every flower is showing a soul blossoming,
enlightening my heart and says how colourful is my life.

Those yellow leaves show me, how lovely it is to let dead things
go.
One more learning old means, not you are going to low. Your
rustling yet showing sprightly life.
So, live this life vigorously and try to spread happiness and after
don't expect.

Psithurism – The sound of rustling of leaves

Long Hugs and Wet Shoulders

Anushka Jain

The soft alcove of your hug,
I cannot breathe
Like I had been doing before
There's an itch I need to scratch
But it's better this way.

You asked me to throw away
The bouquet of cloves
So, I strung cinnamon on barbed wires
Hiding our faces behind each other's shoulders
I like crying without being seen
I like crying while being held.

The silver toes of midnight
Trip upon our endless musings
Legs crossed, arms wide,
Sitting on the cracked faux leather
Exposing something much more tender.

You said how it's been an eternal night
And I've been wondering
What your moon tastes like.
Turn around we'll stitch wings upon our backs
Weave them of the steam of our lives.

Oh! Won't you play your guitar again,
If I make you some hot chocolate?
Aimless gyration
Arms on arms
The smell of petroleum in our nostrils
Don't worry, it's the new tar.

So, we leave the sorrows chasing themselves
Climb haystacks
Upon haystacks
Crack the dried leaves,
Scream vindication!

Oh, my dear,
For goodness's sake
Do you really not know,
How can you really not know
that the moon tastes like vanilla yoghurt?

Why Nature Poems?

Anisha Jain

I'm not saying nature will heal you
The cure, after all, depends on the nature of the wound
But being near a tree can give you oxygen anew

Which really isn't much of a breakthrough
When inside your mind, you know you're doomed
So even if it could, nature won't heal you

But you're so exhausted there's nothing you can do
Cry and relate to the songs that melancholy singer crooned
But unlike a tree, it won't give you oxygen anew.

What's wrong with planning a little rendezvous
With the sunset flowers in the park that have bloomed
Don't expect healing— nature can't do that to you

But the colour of that butterfly can blot out your blue
Even if temporarily, it'll pull out the endless thread of gloom
And bonus: the trees will give you oxygen anew.

This dusky horizon that the sun dips into
Can't replace your shrink; without a ship, you're marooned
Stars, animals, nature—it's not their job to heal you
But that tree can surely give you oxygen anew.

This Little Love of Mine

Hiya Shah

There was a day when I lived
Just because I made a promise,
A promise to never hurt my family,
A promise to never see them cry because of me.
That day seems so long ago,
Those thoughts seem so unknown,
For the sky never seemed pretty,
For the stars, just some lights.
Now, today, I can happily say,
I love someone with all my heart,
And I love myself, each and every part.
The moon seems to smile with me,
The stars seem to dance in joy,
For I found the one,
The one my heart was wanting.
Every milestone we hit,
Every page we turned,
Started with a phone call,
And built a box full of memories.

Stranger

Sharon Paul

A note to the Perfect Stranger whom my eyes had met:
Wandering unknown of your existence,
lost in my own world I went.
Suddenly our eyes had met,
and time seemed to be frozen and set.
A connection so deep, had never been felt,
Wish we could have stopped and met.
And here I sit alone, while the sun sets,
Thinking of you, yet.
The memory keeps coming and makes me regret,
why hadn't I stopped walking and talked,
Just makes me upset
To feel and relive the moment over and over
is a magical fret,
My heart yearns to meet you, to see you again
Well, maybe, sometime in the future ahead.

Mi Amor

Sharon Paul

Dedicated to a secret beloved

A breath of fresh air,
My morning's delight
And my last thought,
Of the daybreak and night.

You feel like home,
My safe haven
You feel like peace,
My soul is craving.

You are my solace,
In turbulent times.
You are my solace,
In happier chimes.

To see you,
Is my day's delight.
Await as I,
For just one sight.

Maybe not destined,
To be together.
But you will be my,
Always and forever.

The weight of my memories

Zubaida Ifshan

As I grow old, the weight of my past burdens me
My body is drenched in the ink of my memory.

Every day I become a stranger to myself
I discover new places hidden inside me, coloured with rotten
memories and sour lullabies, that no longer hush me.

I remember places I have never been to and faces that I have
never seen
Nostalgia takes me to a strange place—I call it home.

But one day when the cage could no longer hold these birds
All the birds would fly away
And someday when the pieces of my past shall fill me
And life could no longer contain me
I, too, would fly away.

On Finding Comfort in Simple Things

Zubaida Ifshan

While I was reading Camus, I inadvertently noticed my dressing table covered in dust, the layer of dust so thick that the flowers carved on it were no longer visible. So, I called my sister and asked her to clean it. She bought a tissue paper and began cleaning. But this moment, which felt so ordinary, soon transformed into such an extraordinary moment that now I feel an urge to write about it. When I saw my sister doing her work, it felt as if she was drowning in this air of innocence awake, but in a reverie, her dreamy humming overflowed my room and choked me. Her comfort and happiness derived from this simple activity took me to a hallucinating labyrinth of memory, to a time when I, too, was happy. Through her eyes, I could see my eyes in the mirror; my happiness seemed like a distant mirage in front of her eyes that gleamed with happiness.

When did the distance between me and my happiness increase so much? Probably when I failed to find comfort in daily chores or when I began to search for this insidious complexity that could never be achieved. These delicate threads of time had crafted such a simple yet complex moment, in which I found myself completely strangulated and she felt free until she bumped her head and sighed, I laughed.

Alone

Tanmay Agrawal

Wondering under the starry night,
Resting alone with my thoughts,
As the man is walking on the moon,
I wonder here—who's mine?

As the years pass,
As the seasons change,
As the glaciers melt,
I wonder here—who's mine?

As I turn the pages of time,
I see myself happy or sad,
With different people at different times,
And I wonder here—who's mine?

Sometimes people come really close,
And again, they go far away,
Like light comes and goes with the shadows,
And I wonder here—who's mine?

Laughing with different people,
Crying with different,
And finally, the day ends,
And I wonder—who's mine?
Having relationships with different people,
Disowning different,
And as the night changes,
I wonder here—who's mine?

Acquaintances become besties,
And besties become enemies,
And at the end of the day,
I wonder here—who's mine?

Every moment is spent with a new person,
Every moment is different,
And the inner me asks to myself,
I wonder here—who's mine?

And as I see the sun rising now,
as the warmth touch my skin,
The sleepy me asks myself,
I wonder—who's mine?

What do I possess?

Tanmay Agrawal

'What is worth living for...
What do I possess?'
Asked the kid

One man replied—
'You possess clothes,
You possess a house,
You possess utensils,
A vehicle to drive.'

'You possess a bed,
And a chair of pine,
You possess shoes,
And food to dine.'

'Almirah full of crockery,
A bar full of Wine,
Expensive paintings on the walls,
And a watch to check the time.'

'You possess some wealth,
Some silver and some gold,
Some small coins of copper,
And notes with neat folds.'

The unsatisfied kid thought—
Life doesn't depend on materialistic things,
As they belong to no one,
They change their owners frequently,
And are left in the living world.

They break or get lost,
Get outdated or rot,
They are rented or are spent,
This is for what they are meant.

The kid moved on and met another man.
He asked the man—
'What is worth living for...
What do I possess?'

The man replied—
'In life you possess relationships.
Relation as a friend.
Relation as a brother.
Relation as a son.
Relation as a mother.'

'Relations stay even after you die.
Those people cry for you
For not to say goodbye.'

'They are there for you,
Day and night,
Standing behind you,
For every fight.'

'They are there for you,
To guide you,
Day and night,
To chide you.'

'Their love is like a river,
To Quench your thirst
Feel the eternal life
Be in there immersed.'

The kid still unsatisfied
Thought—
Relationships are still not permanent,
They are just your memories with someone,
You have a bond together,
And you name the bond.

People are selfish,
Thinking of their good,
Profiting for their business,
Leaving you in deep dark woods.

They break trust,
They use people,
They put on their friendly masks,
And then leave you broken out there.

Some bonds are special,
They are not deceptive,
But one day they leave you,
Out there alone to live.

They give love and care.
But still, they are not my possessions.
You can't just live for people,
As they leave you one day.

It's truth that one day,
This relationship will end.
The strings will stay connected soul to soul,
But is the rest of life a waste.
Still not worth living for.'

The child thought and moved on—

On his way he found another man—
He asked the man—
'What is worth living for...
What do I possess?'

The old man laughed.
And replied—
'What you possess in life are lessons,
You possess experiences,
You possess in life—a life.'

You possess a life,
A life to live,
A life to dream,
A life to survive.

A life to sustain,
A life to cherish,
A life to maintain,
A life to perish.

A life to give,
A life to donate,
A life to earn,
A life to mate.

A life to live,
Live its fullest.

You keep materialistic possessions,
Possession you think you own,
But they are just a part of life,
You don't know when they are gone.

They are small fragments of life,
Fragments you experience,
Experiences you abide,
You abide by experience to win in life.

You experience relations,
Relationships you love,
The love you cherish,
As a milky white dove.

But people are meant to leave,
So, live every moment the fullest,
The fullest so you never regret,
To get another moment to live.

Life is not meant to be long,
But it's meant to be big,
Big enough to satisfy you,
You and your needs.

Live your life just for you,
For nobody will live it for you,
But don't be selfish but be selfless,
Selfless work is key to heaven, it's true.

Always help others,
Without any expectations,
Life will pay you back,
Back to you for generations.

Life is an ocean,
Ocean of love and selflessness,
Just do your part,
And you will be blessed.'

Stand Up

Tanmay Agrawal

Wipe those tears,
Broaden your chest,
Stand up for yourself,
You can't be oppressed.

With a shine in your eyes,
With your head facing the sun,
Stand up for your own rights,
And make the oppressor burn.

Glory in your smile,
What you did was right,
Stand up for yourself,
Wake up now and fight.

We fighters, do not regret,
Now shoot your confident dart,
Stand up for your own rights,
And believe in your pure heart.

Tiny beating hearts,
Uncountable thoughts,
Stand up for yourself,
Don't make thy Mort.
Your age doesn't define you,
Lure yourself for justice,
Stand up for your own rights,
Don't always go for armistice.

You live in Liberty,
What do you fear?
Stand up for yourself,
And make yourself clear.

People choose their own fate,
You eat what you harvest,
Stand up for your own rights,
Let God handle the rest.

Comfy Lines

Deepika Kumari

Bubbles of detergent
dancing in the air,
Become the agent of
smile and glare.

Just reserve a day,
Visit the Sand dunes,
Bluewater or a bay.

Gobbles make you satisfy,
Get vanish to the land of
French or Chocosfy.

Caramelised drink
Makes you think
About comfy nap, or
Milder Blink.

Sparing time for yourself,
Helps you heal,
You know what is real,
You know, what you feel.

Kids want the toys,
Grab them, they want the
Best Popeyes.

Try to thrush,
In this deadly rush.

Never leave your smile,
Without this diamond,
You are Futile.

Your comforts are your pills,
Chew that, sip blues and
Drowse in your bills.

Solace in the Rain She Found

Abhisha Gulati

With her eyelids open wide,
Descended a liquid sunshine
Touching her dewy lips on the side
As if she was a beautiful rhyme

It seemed as if for the lady
the rain itself took a pause
Waiting for her smile
To slowly bloom by her jaws

Her eyes had a spark,
A spark incomparable
A spark whose grace
Made everything seem operable

With each raindrop pelting down her body,
She felt it in her nerves
Solace is what she found
And what she deserves.

Peace

Ammarah Safaa

I watched myself drowning in sorrow
Trembling, with no hope left to borrow
And on the inside, hopeless and hollow.

I saw the fragments in your eyes like stories to find,
Some of them surely blew my mind.

As love grew in the deepest corners of our hearts,
I seem to have evolved in my art.

I found solace, in the way you tie my lace,
I found peace, seamlessly dropping from your hands, and
running through my body,
Like it is where it deserves to be.

Solace

Akanksha Badu

Colours spring out from the vivid smoke
Outrageously bleached dreams make the faint colours seem
bright
They move, so lucid and bleached
Yet I find my eyes caught up in their plainness
Inattentive to the diversity which surrounds it
The ocean that stands still above my head seems holy now
For the angel that swiftly floats through it blesses my eyes.

What lies above me feels divine,
A spectrum of haze, rays of sunshine, the slow fade,
And the scattered pearls that she leaves behind as she
disappears into nothingness
Here, I feel blessed
Here, I find my solace.

What Am I Doing?

Vivek Chowthri

Day by day, I was trying
Only to get caught in the frying
Of the vast work lying
In front of me praying
To complete with naysaying
Which always makes me feel like dying
When no one tried buying
What I have to say without prying
And then there I was crying
When all my hopes started drying
Then came a moment flying
Towards me with a chance of relying
As if my mind was relaying
My thoughts to it without delaying
Then swiftly, I started claying
My plans for future playing
It was all along laying
On my mind throughout the journey flaying
My actions—all I had to do was stopping
And ask
What am I doing?

My Undying Companion

Vivek Chowthri

O! My Undying Companion
Lying in the compact canyon
You've made my life a misery
Filled with a recurring history
Pressured drowsy nights I slept
All your feelings, within, you kept
My failures made me cry
You're the one who made me try
Situations, to me, they lie
That's when I want to die
You always made me stop
Help me in going forward, marching hop
People call you, "Computer"
But you're my sorrow commuter
O! My Undying Companion.

You Will Come and You Will Go

Sidharath Ghassi

Is there a reason? I wonder why
You fade away the marks of my past
As I walk down the shore
It's you whom I follow
With every rising tide, you swallow
Those marks that make me hollow.
You will come and you will go
But I'll stay there forever
See you slowly rise and fall strong
Its life and it works so
It's beautiful to see you come
When the white dress fades in
Crushing, crunching, and hitting the stones
Leaving them in a place where they cannot move
Quietly and slowly, you go
Leaving what you brought on the shore
I wait for you as I count till ten
And here you are again with a new face since then

What should I call you now?
Now you have changed my marks, because
You will come and you will go
But I'll wait for you to come again
I remember the shine and splash
That made me walk on the hot sand
To get a perfect picture of you
You in different band
I knew you would come again
For the sound of your voice, I'll take the pain
Beautiful as first my words in vain
Touching my feet as I lay down in clay
Rising up my body hugging me straight.
It's time for you to go
I knew you won't stay
For once I'll go with you
In the middle pass through many you
And when I'll find the real you,
I'll set my sail upon you, for
You will come and you will go
I'll stay at the shore waiting for you some more.

Not Today

Riya Prasad

Standing in front of the mirror, I loathe myself
For the bit of fat on my stomach,
The moles covering my face
And for not being "pretty" enough.
It is that time of the year again,
Where I look into the mirror and find
Only flaws and inadequacies.
How people around me are doing wonders and I'm not,
How they know so much, and I don't.
I narrow my eyes and say to my reflection, 'Not today.'

And I walk away,
Remembering how I am doing enough as long as I am not
stationary,
How I am enough, for I have conquered the biggest problem life
has thrown at me: a life-threatening disease with which I live
today.
I battle it every day,
And if that isn't brave or enough, I don't know what is.
How I am more than this shell that I call my body.
No one has the consent to make me feel "small".
Not today.
Not ever.

That day

Mitali Kushwaha

We hardly knew each other till that day,
When we met in that journey that way,
Our flocking eyes got stuck for a moment,
And I knew no one else was the reason you were there.
A chilly morning yet to get bright,
I was in black and you in white,
I was following you during the trip that day,
I knew no one else was the reason I was there,
Unknown city unknown people,
Unknown were we, but still together that day.
While heading for the raison d'être that day,
I enjoyed the ride and the scenery passing my way.

59

I think I was trying to know you that day,
I knew no one else was the reason we were there,
Still unknown city, unknown people,
But I was at ease because you were there.
Slowly steadily we started sharing our ways,
The laughs we shared are in memory to date.
While returning from the tour and finally on my way,
I knew a few more people, but I wanted you to be there.
And now when I am back and far from your way,
I still cherish the moments we shared that day!

Loverboy

Sage

Hey lover boy,
Wow I'm speechless you see
How was I to know, you'll set me free
Took my hand as a joke
Looked at me with love, compassion, and a promise
To put a ring on me, I laughed, how could you compromise for me?

My heart was a rock, stronger than the strongest boulder
Love was for the weak, but you gave me your shoulder and I cried
The night we had met in that old bookstore by Cornelia Street
Is still fresh in my memory like the blood on the newlywed virgin's sheet
Your songs felt like the most beautiful melody
All stuck in my little mind

It felt like a million little shining stars had just aligned when
your lips met mine
They refused to part, they had to but not for long
I like how you refused to let me go
Even when my father hurled at you
I love the way your heart holds mine
I love how you know exactly what to say whenever the tears
escape my eyes

It's been a long time indeed
9 years to be precise
I found my forever residence in your heart
And your promises came true
Walking down this aisle was not a joke
But with you, life is funny
Life is a mystery, I want to solve
But not without you

So, lover boy, put this ring on me and scream 'I do,'
And let the world know that I'm yours till death do us part or
maybe even beyond
Because this love is something we'll never rue.
All my childhood fantasies came true just for you.

Virus in the Town

Rohit Agrawal

We are scared of a virus
Virus as deadly as a knife,
It's nothing but an agent
Sent by God to change our life.

We should thank this pandemic
Because it gave us a moment to think,
Our "normal" getting changed
Just in a blink.

Since the distant past
We are trying to be the best,
We had never allowed nature
To go and have some rest.

Humans sitting at home
Worrying about their wages,
Animals on road
Free from 'golden' cages.

63

Lesser number of Heart attacks
Lesser accidents for sure,
Time spent with family
Turns out to be the best cure.

Finally, we realised a change
A change that we must bring,
What we actually need to do
Is to do nothing.

You are my sweet solitude

Ramaponni P
‘

Hey you, yes you!
You are my best companion
You are the one I admire the most
You are an elixir of words

You are cool and warm
You are amazing and weird
You are beautiful inside and out
You are my fantasy and my adventure

You make me happy
You make me laugh
You make me cry
You make me emotional

When I touch you, I feel euphoria
When I hold you, I feel refreshed
When I acquire you, I feel excited
When I complete you, I feel content.

65

You make me listen
You make me speak
You make me read
You make me write

You can sustain both day and night
You have different characters and different genres
You and coffee make the best duo
You are my sweet solitude and an escape from reality

You make me learn
You make me think
You make me understand
You make me explore

You make me travel around the world from the place where I
am
I can find you in my living room and couch
I can find you in my bed and wooden cabinets
You just look perfect even though you are out of place
sometimes

I adore you, you inspire me
I cherish you, you nurture me
I enjoy music along with you
You, me, and favourite corner of the house feel like heaven

Hey, you, yes you are my favourite warmth of comfort
Yes, I am talking about you, my dear books
My dear books—I love you
Love for books and reading never ends!

An Escapade

Ishita Rawat

When the sun is blue and its rays are mere beams of
melancholic misery,
When my hand shivers while sketching the silhouette of a dried
periwinkle
I hunt for hope.
When the poetic phrases in my head are ousted by a perpetual
river of pain,
When the words I mutter are silent screams from my strangled
throat
I hunt for hope.
Yet, the day dulls and dulls into an abyss of bleak twilight where
the trees are purple
And their branches bear envious eyeballs of enmity.
I crawl on a lonely road with wild bushes and unpleasant
solitude,
Struggling to search for an escapade.

Swiftly, at dusk, the clock struck seven and a cliché romantic
saviour saved my day.
The roasted almond scoop slightly dripping down the cone
Seemed enough to disrupt the flow of despair through my veins.
Three hours of simply staring at the embellished night sky
Seemed enough to hush the unsolicited hurricane in my brain.

Growing Up

Ishani Mitra

As a youngster, I always thought,
Growing up must be full of enjoyment and whatnot.
Beginning with switching to pens to write,
Then getting solo berths for train rides.
The idea of growing up is the epiphany,
And I would relate to many.
From learning to balance a bicycle,
To balance a chemical equation.
Growing up seems to be a turnout of,
Emotions with tons of repentance.
Tearing the petals of florals was fascinating,
Until it's given in biology labs for dissecting.
Who thought playing with—well—pulleys would pan out to,
Detecting the tension in the strings holding the buckets steady.
Besides these, the one I miss the most.
Is jumping on the big air Mickey mouse balloon,
Every time I visit a fair, staring at it with disappointed hopes.
Missing those old gold days, I recall.
Growing up is full of regrets and nasty tales.

Smeraldo

Deepti Chauhan

I now understand you have shades.
You aren't black and white, nor a mere rainbow
I am trying to look at your insecurities
I am trying to notice your fears.

The look I had earlier was rather plain
But today the colours have painted the sky
Today the moon isn't crying alone, nor is he scared
For the entire sky is embracing him, crying with him.

You are not the beast who has to hide
You are not the one who has to suffocate, so, please
Unleash your worries as to how this world looks at you, for
You are not the one who should succumb himself to his cries.

The hydrangeas are lifeless,
They look glummer than usual
The lone purple poppy is crying too
Maybe, their hearts can feel, your fears due.

That man had a terrible ending
But you're not him.
His love was never realised
His feelings got buried alongside.

I see you now, —a ball of turmoil
Will you let me untangle you?
Will you let me free you
From the labyrinths of your mind?

I'll snap the gates to your
Heart, that's beating slowly
I'll shake him to the extent
He's forced to see the reality.

I'll wipe the rust with my tears
I'll light up that cold castle
I'll wake her up in that era, just
To make sure his love is realised.

I'll walk the Alps or the Kailash
For Zeus to grant me that flower
And this time around,
I'll be standing before you with the bouquet.

Dressed in white and gold, with
The forbidden colossal flower in my hands.
This time around, I'll ask you,
with a tiny smile and a scared face,
'Do you still love me? It's been centuries though.'

I'll free the moon of its eclipse, touching its surface
And looking it in the eye,
The words slowly being released from their chains,
'Mon Amour, you're handsomer than the devil, who rules
desires.'

My forehead touching the clear surface
Of the once rugged moon
My lips breathing, 'Why did you wait?
Why didn't you run before? I've waited so long for you.'

A miracle flowed and drenched the celestial nymph.
The universe which was once barren and silent
Was filled with the cries of the lovers, tied
In an embrace that even fate couldn't intervene in today.

Fate too looked at the pair and said,
'I've been cruel, my darlings,
But I know, the reunion is always sweeter
than any nectar found in nature's bosom.'

Perhaps we were meant to meet this way.
Maybe, that life had nothing in it for us.
But I'm glad, we met in this life.
I'm glad, I found you, Mon Amour.

Grooves and Ridges

Md Adnan

Hands—
Firmly clutched,
With efforts engraved
On the fingers that touched.
Yet, slipping through
The sands rushed.
And all that stays
Are curves on the surface.

These curves are the creases
Of the past
Of which, moments have been lived
And only memories are, that last.

These curves are the soils
For the sprouts of growth,
Where chirping expectations witness
The blossoms of hope

These curves are the promises
Of withstanding the gales of change
And the symbols of trying,
Getting better as the years pass.

And just like these curves remain
And trod on the skin,
On and on
Continues the age-old tale.
Each time imprinting a different essence
On time's unprecedented trail.

But there is still much to come
And there is still much to go.
For there stands a vast road
Midst time's continuous flow.

And if this thing called life
Is so very long,
How about an "us"
An "us" that's lifelong?

Then never will there be any parting.
Those 'byes' will
No more be 'good'.
And along the walk of our life
We will tread together.
A walk where
The grooves of your palm
Eternally rest
On the ridges of mine.

The Version of Me

Akhila James

There's a version of me somewhere deep within
A version who doesn't care about inhibition or chaos
An image that befriends vulnerabilities and finds solace in
letting go
An image of me who considers anxiety as a just warning and
perfections as mere fantasy. Never tongue-tied, never scared.
A person with raw instincts, unafraid to fall in love.
An emotional mess, both good and sad. Far from ideal, closer to
mad.
A person with hope in her eyes, unafraid to trust kindness. A
person unhinged and near "insane"
My inner child, who still believes in humanity and feelings
An inner soul who longs to live life relentlessly and seeking.
I wonder who she is, but more importantly, I wonder how she's
doing
I understand now, probably happy and free, carefree about
demeanour or degree.

Probably living life on instincts, feelings and "making the move", despising regret and avoiding "what ifs"

Unafraid to be real and not making up versions of herself to please the crowd

But I'm not ready to meet her. Unfortunately, as of right now, she seems intimidating

She is me without constraints. She is me without fear. As of right now, she lives in my head.

She is me buried deep within. She is me, longing to see the world through me.

Nobody knows her except for me. I wonder if she knows about me.

But I'm hoping to meet her, cry with her, laugh with her.

I'll talk to her till the sun comes up and finally, we will have things in common to talk about

We'll be best friends who always see the best in each other, charismatic and effortless

Best friends who always understand each other, never toxic, never fake

Never jealous and never vain.

And finally, we will be one. The ultimate reunion of me and my own. The love story the world is so desperate in need of. A story of self-love, peace, and acceptance.

Theme of Solitude

Anagha Gopan O.G.

The humming of the voice
A walk through the mind
Parenting the dreams and thoughts
Fumigating the ego
Searching for selfless love
Nurturing the peace and glory
Breathing deep into solitude

The End

Anagha Gopan O.G.

Amidst worldly pleasures
A journey with clear route
A genuinely desiring attitude.
A clear vision towards the end
Where the end is the beginning.
Consoling, reconstructing, and admiring
So as to not dwindle.
Escapism towards freedom
From worst ever
Gluing the positives and negatives
Making everything neutral
Wrecked pieces of mind
Stabilizing the inner and outer
Welcoming peace and glory.

My Universe, My Muse

Anju Kurien

I never missed any chance
To visit that place.
That castle had much to tell me
That untold mystery
Blurred my vision
Clenched my fist
Inside my heart, yet
The castle inspired me
Under the green tent
I had too much think about
Intertwining
Of my reality and fantasy
I dreamt too much
Lingering around this place.
But I never knew that
This place in real is going to gift me
With something that will always
Urge me to realise those dreams.

I never knew
In a blink of an eye
I am going to have a gaze
At 'my Universe'!
My Universe lent me hands
And I've got hold on them.
In no time happened
That amazing blend of
My colours with my Universe!

Wonders do exist!
Once you start looking at them
With awe and passion
They will never cease to amaze you.
Just like your dreams!
Start dreaming and crave for them.
My palette gave colours
To my Universe
My Universe, my muse, my passion
I fell in love with my muse
The elixir of my life.

Scent of an Anonymous

Dr. Arun Kumar Shastri

Now you live in my memory only
Your scent, your touch and
Your shining head, the glowing
Marble skin, vibrates continuously
In my heart, in my soul.
I was not aware of you before
That you exist on earth somewhere
But all of a sudden you were the,
Most important person for me
I feel lucky that you met,
Our separation within twenty-four hours
Was the most uncomfortable span of my life
Thoughts of you are wandering, encircling around
My mind in and out. If you loved me
Or not, I do not care as those few minutes
One cannot consider enough for love
To emerge or sprout up, but
How much your scent bothered me
Is the point to ponder here? And is the main
Things to consider.
It was long, long ago in the valley of gardens
Near Mountain Alps and flowing river
All I remember vaguely then.

But the closest is your body fragrance you scent,
Yes, I don't say, but to admit, your body
Scent, the day we met and departed, that
was your last day in Switzerland
hope you remember, of course you do, I guess
For God's sake it is not a guess, but
I am confident as you started living in me.
We found none that day when we lost
Our way in the woods, you saw me
Shouted for help down the hill,
The first few calls went echoed in the woods.
Then I became conscious, some human is calling
I started stepping down but slipped
Straight into your arms.

Then we both rolled down up to many
Feet on a snowy slope.
I was under you, and you were on me, then
You were under me, and I was on you
It repeated many times we forgot
Till we came to stop against a heavy bush.
We didn't mind getting up as we were lost
So, in the sudden flash of events happening
And so amazed and mesmerised that
We forgot to realise pain bruises and swollen
Knees ankles arms and heads

I never asked you to get up
And you never pushed me aside to
Make me feel so
We lay there for many moments,
Exhausted and unaware
Of each other relishing that we are alive
And safe though hurt, and then we realised
Each other company and started enjoying it
Oh my god oh my god, we laughed yes, we did laugh
We found none around us we did not bother
To have somebody near us
That day we loved to be as such when we lost.
Now you live in my memory only
Your scent, your touch and
Your shining head, the glowing
Marble skin, vibrates continuously
In my heart, in my soul.
I was not aware of you before
That you exist on earth somewhere.

From Eve to Eve

Deborah Mejía

Soft is all I ever feel
When I touch your cheek
And we sleep at ease
In the cooling breeze
Of coming winter freeze
Feathers, pillows, warm, still,
From all these feelings I can't pick
Which side of you makes my heart beat
At this moment that won't repeat?
Just breathe, breathe,
Going soft as our eyes meet

Light-headed, my thoughts spiral down
Into the inner conjurings of my brain,
Which amuses itself easily
Imagining multi-coloured beings
And immortal toads
While I try to put the cereal box
Back inside the fridge
And the warmth of my bed
Chases me back to sleep

At night, among synths and beats,
The neon becomes your own glow
And I'm transported back home,
Rekindling all that I missed
The sounds that made me sway
Hum in all the right ways
As the kitchen serves as a stage
With rhythms from every age
And melodies our heart syncs
Now we twirl at the brink
Of becoming one love
With the music we dream of

Love so sweetening,
A whole day of reminiscing
Goodbye so sickening…
Awaiting the next meeting

Your Breath Wills the Seasons to Life

Deborah Mejía

You're the dew that sprinkles flowers,
Frees their fragrance in the air,
Trailing the scent of life born anew
When the taste of spring,
With its sweet honey of hope,
Blossoms forever on your plum petal lips,
Blooming with a fluttering smile

And with the rain comes you
As tears unleash when your eyelashes meet
A fan of raindrops and vaporous heat
Dripping with silent passions
Which kiss our skins, shower the ground
You are the spring that comes around,
The warm summers and cool autumn breeze…

When the moon brings the harvest
And the sun rises over orchestral fields,
Yellows and purples fill me to the brim
While my soul sings nature back into me

I dress myself with the colours
Of the skies high above,
Cover myself in its freedom
As I free-fall up to you, an inviting home
Where I sing with the voice of mountains,
Laugh with the power of the seas,
And I run swift with the river
Alas, I become spring

Fairy Tale Words

Deborah Mejía

The sweetest of whispers,
The caress of ink over paper,
The worlds that I create:
That is where you and I meet

Made straight out of fiction,
Born from my heart,
You are the love of my life

The Musings of Rivit

Anindita Chatterjee

Hello there, beautiful! (I am not such a big fan of using pronouns, so all of you, welcome aboard this crazy space, because mind you, things are just going to get crazier.)

Looks like you are here to engage in some nonsensical, over-hyped, cliché school of thought. I will try my very best not to offend any of your sentiments, your parents'-imposed sentiments, your forefathers or foremothers-imposed sentiments, your societal-shaped sentiments; to be very soundly clear, I am going to raise some observational lifestyle issues that you (or some of you again) perceive, feel, despise, and have the urge to speak out your mind and say it aloud, but alas!

All these years we have been trained to just "think before we speak" (apologies, this dyslexic, 18-year-old champ is a little slow in comprehending accurate idioms.)

So, without further ado, let's begin with this madness

1) INCEPTION OF OUR PERSONALITY: *The rollercoaster ride of being "ascribed" to our parents and being a "proud" entrant to the "most respected" two lineages of forefathers, foremothers. Isn't that a wholesome feeling?*

So, my growth development from the onset of my infancy-childhood-adolescent to finally adulthood was very weird, nostalgic, beautiful, comforting, sad, awful, and nerve-wracking… this list of expressing emotions through adjectives won't end.

I always used to proudly claim that I was an extraverted person who, in her childhood days, had no shame to dance in front of the public, speak and debate like Atal Bihari Vajpayee Ji (India's ex-Prime Minister), hum on Deepika Padukone "Hare Krishna Hare Ram" tacky song (realising much later what those lyrics actually meant *cringe*) and thinking that studying in school only comprised of me engaging with my friends, sharing lunch and coming back home to act like my teacher, don a dupatta, and teach in front of my mini-blackboard with chalks to a bunch of toys and imaginary people, Ah good ol' days…

Well, I realised much later that I was sent to school to actually learn, re-learn, perform, get rewarded, be promoted and again learn, re-learn etcetera for all those 14 years of my school life. I am not saying that it did not shape me as a person and I did not gain knowledge about the mechanism of this working, egocentric world where imagination, and creative ideas are derailed with mind-numbing, rote-learning techniques.

Friendships. Ever heard of that one? To be really honest with you, I never had a best friend, only friends and classmates, I couldn't understand the concept of 'BFF Foreva,' I used to cry and have that tinge of loneliness when I was not given the chance to be part of a close-knit group (especially the popular ones) but they were the ones that made your life miserable with self-esteem issues regarding diaspora of subjects not limited to body shaming, social skills, popularity, teacher's pet, poor performance in studies, arrogance, extra clingy behaviour, too soft-spoken, dumb wit and so on.

My school life has been enveloped with a fair amount of good and bad days, but what I did learn out of this 14-year rollercoaster ride is that no one, and I mean nobody, should be given the power of your happiness, your thoughts, and opinions. Learn from my experience and do not pay heed to the people who judge you for the way you are. You are a beautiful creation of this world, created by some unknown force who has given you this chance to lead your life your own way. Never ever let hypocritical snakes that will swim in every phase of your life wield this power, steer clear, and you are good to go for this wholesome experience called life. Choose your companions wisely, you cannot foresee your future or rewind the past, but you can control the present, start now! (I know it's easier said than done, but the sooner you take the charge of your life into your own hands and lead it the way you want to, the happier you will be.)

Let's revisit some of our old memories in school (The Indian education system, to be more precise), especially pertaining to the 'anxious' period for all school-goers (future dumplings- you have no idea what's on your way, friends).

Boards! The major highlight of our school years would possibly be our grade tenth and twelfth board examinations (some of you may have other highlights). Who knew that passing Grade Ten was not just the only relief you get but that one sheet of paper has to be kept with utmost security and safety because, oh well, how will you apply for government documents like Aadhar, Passport, job application, college application etc.? Because that sheet contains our date of birth! (Because apparently, the word of a paper has more importance than our parents' biological audited by-product genetic mutation.)

Who knew that the National Register of Citizens documents would have less importance than the Grade Ten mark sheet? (Well, now I can only hope that this line doesn't get me to jail cause if comedians, actors, activists can't get easily away with their so-called 'constructive' or 'humorous' criticism then who am I, an 18-year-old champ who likes to state the obvious fact, to remain scotch-free.)

My bad, I have this habit of talking in sub-sub parts about layers of the concerned subject, because there is so much to write about but the least that I can do is just make this simpler for you because honestly, nobody would want to hear this constant rant of a teenager's complex mind thoughts, Will they? Or should we just rely on psychologists or psychotherapists? Don't these mental consultants' celebrated workers have someone alongside them when they need the empathy talks more than concerned people do?

Is it so hard to just for once, not be so calculative, old school brainwashed fellow, and self-centred jerk and just for once reach out to one another who is in dire need of your hug? Is it that hard to not be selfish and just constantly run in this so-called 'maze' of life till you officially get covered with a hound of white sheet covers, wooden planks and fire?

Is it so hard for the school curriculum to include life skill teachings in a simpler manner and make it easier for students to not take stress, anxiety regarding so-called rote learning, peer pressure, teacher's rude behaviour, and gender neutrality? But actually, make them introspect everyday life problems with accurate problem-solving capabilities and sound decision-making?

Can't we humans for once just be really assured and happy and not get jealous about somebody else's triple, quadruple times etcetera contentment than us?

Wouldn't this world be a better place if we could just uphold our own identity and be comfortable in our own skin rather than stigmatising one another?

Let's sum up this thought with a beautiful line: If only heaven wasn't so far away that I could enthral you with my hard-earned achievement of having the strength to be alive in every movement, I will show it to you one day, heaven, I will show it to you.

2) CHOICES: *Pay your money and take your choice, simple philosophy of give and take of decision-making, but is it really that easy?*

When was the last time you had to make a conflicted choice?

I always despised the concept of 'choosing', it's such a twisted concept-to take a fall for your decision because you choose between the two positives, two negatives, one positive and one negative and any other combination of choices.

The one thing I do believe is that choices, to some extent, define your personality, what sort of morals or values do you resonate with or how much egoism or humility a person can sustain in this complex duality of the world.

In these eighteen years of my existence in this world, I started to comprehend the complexities of the world after Grade Four, I would probably be nine years old, so technically speaking, I started to develop this 'conscience' of mine ten years back and I am elated to inform you that it has made me a very grounded person as I am able to acknowledge and be grateful for the finer things in life that the almighty God has been gracious enough to bestow upon me.

Now, I believe that there would be a handful of you who might fall into the category of atheism and agnosticism (don't Google it... I'll share the meanings of these two words; atheism is a belief that can be held by an individual, group, or a community as a whole that there is no existence of God whereas Agnosticism neither believes nor disbelieves in the existence of God.)

I proudly follow the doctrine of Agnosticism because that's my 'choice' to resonate with spirituality as it calms down my anxious mind when I feel lost, hopeless, or simply just in the dire need to have this feeling that other than my parents, there is someone else who supports me and looks after me in every sorrow and happiness. For some of you, this may sound nonsensical, or weird, you might even let out a chuckle by reading this out or just simply say it in your head, 'What a load!' Well, my friend, I won't get offended by your interpretation of this subject because it's your 'choice'.

See? Wasn't that simple? Why do we humans feel the need to 'justify' our 'choices' when we are consciously well aware of our predicaments?

Why do we always have to impose our 'choices' on others just so there can be 'peace' and 'comfort' amongst us and others? Why can't we simply celebrate the fact that our 'choices' not just define our personality but also give us the strength and courage to have an 'individual mind' and have the courage to perform our 'actions' and speak aloud our 'words' with no strings attached?

It's a simple theory, friends, 'Let and do live.' Life is too short to blame another person for your unhappiness, sorrowful or desolate life. You have to take a stand for the past, and present 'choices' that you committed to.

I know it's hard to accept the fact that at the end of the day, whether you lose or gain in this rollercoaster ride of ups-downs, side-swings, cross lanes of life, at least there will be no regrets because of the way you led your life.

3) **CLOSURE:** *The goodbyes are the hardest and yet the most liberating feeling in the world.*

Well looks like I am at the end trail of my book, otherwise I had many subjects to cover up with you, my friends, but don't worry, we'll meet again surely, but only if you feel there is a need to, so I will be waiting for your feedback, rockstars!)

To be fair with you as we part ways, this is my first amateur attempt to write down my feelings through this modicum of a very strange title that I opted out for. I am not some philosopher, or a certified life coach or psychologist. I just wanted to let go of all these feelings and emotions that I had bottled within me for a very long time; so, much appreciation if you came to the end of this line, it really showcases your soft, caring and humane side to read my musings (happy tears).

So, au revoir, friends, until we meet again (I really hope not, though, as sometimes the amount of self-control it takes to say what's on my mind is so immense, I need a nap afterwards.)

Deepest Longings of Guilt

Anindita Chatterjee

If only heaven wasn't so far away that if I could seek forgiveness
of my sin
That run deep-rooted in the shackles of my boundless fervour
ignorance
How could I not fathom my beloved sister's earnestness
Who loved me whole-heartedly despite my arrogance?

Why does my mind follow the beats of chagrined thoughts
When my soul should have expressed sanctity in utmost routs?
Oh, I wish I could rewind that day of misery
The day I lost my sister forever in the wraths of petulant naivety

 I could still hear the wailing of her boundless screams
As she tried to convey the truth with utmost impunity
How could I cloud my ill judgement of her purity
While she was defending against my passive authority?

She was the embodiment of a good disciple
Who aspired to propel in every sphere of her desires.
She had the propensity of being strong-willed
No matter what may befall her endeavours

Though she was mired with patriarchal chains of hollowness
And I 'proudly' propagated the indecisiveness nature of
connivance
She respected the regressive-stricken family laws
And I vehemently professed these prejudiced diktats

I so wish I could revive her laughter and pride back
As I crushed it with my own bare hands of sanity
Not only did I question the 'purity' of her being
But without any hindered thought, choked her to vicious twine

She deserved my respect as a brother
And I impeded it with my bleak masculinity
If heaven wasn't so far away
That I could drown myself in the pool of treacherous saline

Meet the Co-Authors

Abhisha Gulati

Abhisha Gulati is a published poet and a writer who is currently a Psychology major at the University of Delhi. Being a writer for the past 7 years, Abhisha Gulati has crafted more than a hundred poems and many short stories which have been recognised and awarded by several platforms. Her essays and articles have been published in several MUN Magazines.

Akanksha Badu

Akanksha is a third-year sociology student at Jesus and Mary College, University of Delhi. She is a film enthusiast with a keen interest in social issues and mental wellness, as well as international relations. While she writes to express, she hopes her readers find themselves in her words.

Akhila Rajeena James

Akhila is an English major trying to figure out life by finding happiness in the little things in life. She firmly believes that a good poem doesn't necessarily need to have complex words and added sophistication. Instead, it needs to be open communication with oneself.

Ammarah Safaa

Ammarah Safaa is a Dubai-based budding author, poet, artist, and a full-time student pursuing BSc. in Biotechnology. Her work often resolves around love, nostalgia, equality, she loves to utilise her voice by raising awareness against wars. She has performed in many artistic  and cultural events in association with organisations like Rooftop Rhythms.

Anagha Gopan O.G.

 Anagha hails from Thrissur, Kerala, India. She is a Civil Engineering B. Tech graduate from Cochin University of Science and Technology. She has also authored a book named 'Soul Human Interaction'.

Anindita Chatterjee

Anindita Chatterjee, an 18-year-old champ, is currently pursuing her undergrad in Philosophy at Miranda House, Delhi University. She is a single child brought up in a perfect blend of aficionados, hailing from lawyers to armed forces backgrounds, and usually likes to  take charge of her life with nonchalant activities like public speaking, acting and overtly zealous love for music.

Anisha Jain

Anisha Jain is an amateur writer/poet from Delhi. A person of both the sciences and the arts, she is also an engineering student. She was the youngest co-author of Kaleidoscope, a prose anthology. She has a blog with an international readership, Charlie and the Cerebration Factory, where she posts her poems, stories, and write-ups.

Anju Elizabeth Kurien

Anju, a PG scholar of Mar Ivanios College, Trivandrum, Kerala, is a great admirer of art, who seeks self-expression through her drawings and words. Most of her writings accompany her drawings posted on social media platforms. She aspires to create works of art to which her audience could easily connect yet with deeper layers of meaning.

Anushka Jain

Anushka is a high schooler who pens poetry on her small personal blog. She is a long-time contributor to her school magazine and has also been published in an inter-school anthology which was circulated country wide. When she isn't racking her brains over homework or writing poetry, she likes to read on her park's swing, put on some music or try her hands at baking.

Arshpreet Kaur

Arshpreet wrote her first article at the age of seven. Working as a professor, tutor, reader, and successful home manager, she is an ardent lover of nature, and whenever she finds time she is into true solace. At that point in time, she listens to her heart and allows her mind to articulate poems, thoughts etc.

Czarina Datiles

Czarina Datiles is a student who uses writing as a way to express her innermost feelings and thoughts that would otherwise remain stuck within her. A dreamer and an ambitious woman, she strives to publish her very first book. It is through her words that one will truly find her genuine self.

Deborah M. Mejía

Deborah is an agender, panromantic-asexual Honduran writer that has been creating stories in her head in both Spanish and English since even before she could write. She values the importance of artistic storytelling to create mediums of human connection and

strives to bridge differences of race, and beliefs through poetry, and visual arts shared through her social media.

Deepika Kumari

Deepika is a young and budding writer as well as a keen art and craft lover. Currently, she's pursuing her graduation in English Literature. Trivial things of no value carry lots of value for her. Hindi T.V. dramatic shows inspired her to grab the pen.

Deepti Kumari Chauhan

Pursuing B.A. English Honours from the prestigious Delhi University, Deepti's areas of interest include French art and literature, south-east Asian literature and culture and South Asian culture and diversity. "Writing is the solace that mends every pain washed away with or without time."

Dr Arun Kumar Shastri

Dr Arun specialises in psychology, yoga and naturopathy and medical astrology. He firmly believes in the motto' Live and Let Live." His poems revolve around themes like love, nature, friendships, and romance.

Hiya Shah

When she is not writing in her favourite coffee shop, Hiya spends most of her time reading, cooking, travelling the city, and watching her favourite movies. An admitted sports fanatic, she feeds her addiction to Formula 1 by watching Grand Prix on Sunday evenings.

Hrishita Sood

Since childhood, Hrishita has always been very exuberant about writing. She really likes to write about things to which readers can easily relate and is full of emotions, experiences, and opinions of her own.

Ishani Mitra

Ishani is a teenager experiencing various colours of life and penning down the thoughts in her mind. Writing poetries has always been a medium to share her thoughts and emotions with the world. She writes about experiences with which everyone can empathise.

Ishita Rawat

Ishita is a spontaneous teenager who staunchly believes in seizing the moments and cherishing the present. Ishita is a humanities student and money, and market fascinates her. She is devoted to words, finds freedom in poetry, and adores expressing emotions via metaphors and imageries.

Mahek Patel

Mahek is an 18-year-old girl who is learning to appreciate the little things in life. She writes under the pen name 'mystique' which can be interpreted as my-stique meaning my verse or poem. She seeks comfort in her diary by penning down her emotions. She is pretty helpful and a good listener.

Md. Adnan

Adnan is a student of Literature at the University of Delhi. A person whose interests lie in myriad spheres, he is a breathing structure of imperfection who always aims to reconcile his contentedly accepted reality with his transformational imaginations. When it comes to poetry, he considers himself to be an occasional poet who writes only when inspiration precedes intention.

Mitali Kushwaha

Mitali was born and raised in Jabalpur, a humble city of Madhya Pradesh, India. She mostly writes at night when she is off her motherly duties and spends the day partnering with business leaders to manage the human resource department of an MNC. She is building, mending, and  trying to get over every little bit of what life offers, and poetry helps her express it.

Pratishtha Jindal

 Pratishtha is a writer and undergraduate student in B.A. Elective English and History programme at Delhi University. Her areas of interest include gender, the LGBTQIA+ community, and their representation in literature as well as other forms of media. Growing up in a hetero-patriarchal society, she finds researching issues relating to intersectionality as a way to unlearn and re-establish social norms.

Sage

Sage is a fruity Virgo who is obsessed with Taylor Swift and music. She expresses herself in poems and songs.

Ramaponni P

Ramaponni is a budding writer from Chennai and a former HR professional. She likes to learn and explore new things. She always believes that 'Life is all about setting and breaking our benchmarks and not about competing with anyone else, yet we are all part of the race.' She loves reading and aspires to pen down her thoughts straight from her heart.

Rashi Sadhu

Rashi Sadhu is an Independent Investment Consultant. She's on a mission to spread financial literacy. She believes financial freedom should be a vital goal for every common person. Her passion involves writing poetry on real scenarios. She is passionate about the stock market. She is a proud mother and writer (by choice).

Riya Om

Riya is pursuing MBA in finance and working. She belongs to Punjab. She loves reading, writing, and listening to music. She has published two poetry books called "Shayarana Si Hai Yeh Zindagi" and "Mere Ehsas". She loves to make friends and live life.

Riya Prasad

Riya Prasad can usually be found reading a book, and that book will more likely than not be a fiction fantasy. Writing has always been her passion and go-to when she feels low. She is particularly fond of writing poetry, which has helped her cope with these uncertain times. Her  writing is focused on the discovery of the various aspects that make up the self.

Sharon Paul

 Sharon is a student of English Literature at Jesus and Mary College, New Delhi. She is an avid reader, ardent romantic and art lover. To her, poetry is a way of venting her overflowing emotions. Faith and Family and Love are her priorities. If you're looking for her, you may certainly find her in her room, nose deep into yet another Novel.

Sidharath Ghassi

An engineer, researcher, and MBA by profession. A pet parent, a loving husband, and an introvert by discipline. 

Tanmay Agrawal

Tanmay Agrawal is an aspiring author. Belonging from Samastipur, a small district of Bihar, India. He is a student and has a passion for writing since childhood. He is looking forward to contributing as much as he can to the world.

Vivek Chowthri

Vivek is an engineer and an aspiring filmmaker. His previous book was a fantasy mystery story named "The Phantom Magician and The Tiger Palace". He wrote his first poem in XI Grade. Stories, poems, and movies were the only things which kept him energetic from the "pressure cooker" environment during his higher secondary schooling.

Zahistha Begum R

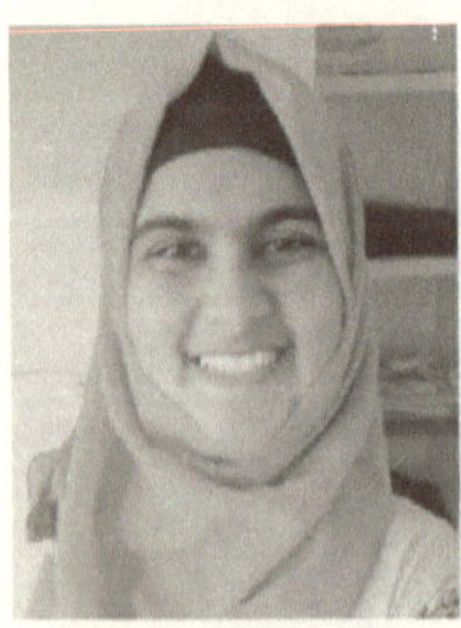

Zahistha Begum, 20, is an amateur artist, nutritionist and now a budding poet. Being an artist for the past 3 years, her literary talents got provoked by the urge of her paintings to spill out the words. Now, she hopes to explore and indulge in this endless joy of the literary world.

Zubaida Ifshan

Zubaida Ifshan is an undergraduate student of Jesus and Mary College, University of Delhi pursuing English and History. She loves to read and write poetry.

Rohit Agrawal

Rohit Agrawal is an MBA from IIM Calcutta with a major interest area centring around strategy and finance. He is working as a consultant at Bain & Co. Apart from his professional life, he likes penning down his thoughts in his free time as he believes that the power of words is unparalleled.

INKFEATHERS PUBLISHING

India's Most Author Friendly Publishing House

Stay updated about the latest books, anthologies, events, exclusive offers, contests, product giveaways and other things that we do to support authors.

 Inkfeathers Publishing

 @InkfeathersPublishing

 @_Inkfeathers

 @Inkfeathers

 Inkfeathers.com

We'd love to connect with you!